ANSELM B

What did the first Christians believe?

Leslie Houlden

Lecturer in New Testament,
King's College, London

LUTTERWORTH PRESS
Guildford, Surrey

For my Godchildren

First published 1982

ISBN 0-7188-2515-2

Set in 11/12pt. Bembo
Printed in Great Britain by
Lonsdale Universal Printing Ltd.,
Salisbury Road, Larkhall, Bath, Avon.

Contents

1. What about believing?

2. What about the first Christians?

3. What did they believe about Jesus?

4. What did they believe about God?

5. What did they believe about themselves?

6. What did they believe about their present?

7. What did they believe about their future?

8. What did they believe about the church?

9. What did they do about worship?

10. What did they believe about right and wrong?

11. What does it matter what they believed?

The editors say . . .

Anselm Books are written specially for lay people who want to think about their faith. They will help explore important matters of Christian belief and action.

Each books deals with a single question—about God, or Jesus Christ, or the Church, or the Bible, or prayer, or bringing up children in the faith, or marriage, or abortion, or euthanasia, or the use of nuclear power . . .

Why *Anselm*? Anselm was a great Christian scholar of the eleventh century who became Archbishop of Canterbury. The original title in English of one of his best known books was *Faith Seeking Understanding*.

Peter Baelz
Dean of Durham Cathedral

Jean Holm
Lecturer in Charge of Religious Studies,
Homerton College, Cambridge

1
What about believing?

Suppose we went on a journey together or spent a long evening in each other's company. We might come to talk about what we *really believed*.

What should we be talking about? Should we not be talking about what we thought of life, about what was worth aiming for, about the best way to plan our society, about God, about right and wrong? If we talked long about these deep subjects, we should soon find that we had enough in common to talk about them with sympathy for each other; but we should also find that at points we disagreed. We believed different things and believed in different ways. If we already knew each other, but had not talked like this before, that might surprise us, because we thought we had a lot in common. We were both from the same kind of school or district, were both Christians, both supported the same political party. Yet here we were, disagreeing at all sorts of points in our discussion.

I said we should almost certainly disagree, not just about *what* we believed, but also about *how* we believed. We should begin by noticing the 'what'. You were in favour of capital punishment and I was against it. But after a time we should be aware also of the 'how'. You were always looking for evidence to back your beliefs, I gave more weight to my feelings. Each of us would probably end up by being astonished at the other. How could somebody think like *that*? And if we were very tolerant, we might be delighted at the richness of the human mind.

If we met another time, it might occur to us to ask why and in what ways we disagreed so much, despite all that we held in common. What should we put forward as the reasons? Or rather, where should we look for answers? It would not be long before we started comparing our backgrounds in some detail: what sort of people our parents were, what schools we went to, who had influenced us, what churches we belonged to, what books we read, and then, if we could see clearly enough, what fantasies and hopes and fears jostled together deep down in our minds. We might have to admit that some of these things, which we scarcely recognised or perhaps scarcely liked to recognise, played a great part in forming the way we believed.

So we believe differently from each other. But we do not just believe anything we like. However much we feel in charge of what we believe and have truly thought it out, we have been formed by all sorts of influences: our psychological make-up and our family, our nation and our social group, our education in the widest sense of the word. All these things form us gently and, for the most part, without our knowing it; though sometimes we feel them all too keenly, maybe react against them and reject what they prompt us to believe. We renounce the faith (or the unbelief) of our parents and come to the opposite position, for reasons partly clear and good, partly mysterious and almost beyond our control. Or else some powerful experience, like a love affair or a bereavement, or an overwhelming force, perhaps from some small source like a poem or a picture or a speech, affects us. It shakes up all our beliefs and makes us look at everything in a new way. We call it conversion. As a result, we are aware of our beliefs more intensely than before—and are probably less able to appreciate the beliefs of those who differ from us. We are also likely to be blind to the undoubted continuity between our old and our new beliefs.

There is another way in which we do not believe anything we like. Suppose that on that long journey your companion was not somebody you knew, was not somebody who, at any rate on the surface, shared much of your background. Suppose he was someone from a different culture or (magic carpet provided) a different age. Assuming (more magic) that you found a way of overcoming difficulty over language, you would at first have much more of a problem in sharing your beliefs. There would seem to be much less common ground. In the earlier case, you might feel that, though you disagreed with your friend, it would not be quite beyond imagining for you to believe as he believed. But now you might well say to yourself, 'I could never in a million years believe *that.*'

There are things we are simply not in a position to believe, even if we cannot easily say why. For example, we are unable to believe (as people have believed) that the earth is a kind of dish resting on the backs of a number of indescribably large elephants, though we might find it hard to assemble evidence against such a belief. Again, it is not a live option for us to believe in the gods of ancient Greece, however familiar we might be with the stories about them. Yet how many of us could say exactly why we take them to be creatures of human imagination? We are shaped and limited by the culture we live in. It makes us see things in a certain way, or in a limited range of ways, and it cuts us off from seeing them in other ways. We can, it is true, become self-conscious about it, criticise, modify or make allowance for it, but we can never get outside of it.

Of course our own culture's way of seeing things did not appear the other day, all fresh, out of the blue. It is the result of an immense process of development, ages long—a slow movement of habits, ideas, beliefs, interlocking with each other and moving into each other. In a word, it is a *tradition.* We believe what we believe largely because we are the product of such a tradition, or, more likely, a number of distinguishable traditions (religious, artistic, literary, national, local). They have all gone to make up what we are and what beliefs we hold.

Yet to this massive, complex stream, each of us makes his own contribution. Each is his own brand new amalgam of characteristics and thought, close to crowds of others of course, but unique, and, to those who care enough for us to notice and to listen, fascinating. There is much to be said for church creeds that begin 'I believe'. Each of us believes for himself, however much he is indebted to others of past and present, and each of us needs to know it and to say it.

Believing involves being one with others but also being different. It involves taking from the past and receiving what is given to us. It also involves accepting its invitation and walking along its path.

2
What about the first Christians?

All that we have said in the last chapter is preliminary to our subject. If this was true about *our* believing, it may also be true about early Christians and *their* believing. Let us pick up the important points.

The first Christians did not drop from heaven ready-made. They were part of the world of their time. They inherited its tradition and shared its culture. They believed many things that were older than Christianity and came into it with many of their beliefs already formed. Their new faith did not simply erase all these beliefs, however much it transformed them.

While some of those beliefs were common currency at the time (e.g. the belief in angels or spirits of various kinds), others were special to one group or another. Most Christians, especially in the first years, had been brought up as Jews, but that does not mean that they had all their beliefs in common. Judaism at that time was full of diversity. It was widely spread in the countries around the Mediterranean and the Jews were affected by the cultures alongside which they lived. They also differed and formed groups among themselves, such as the Pharisees and Sadducees whom we meet in the gospels (e.g. Mark 12:13, 18), and the Essenes who wrote the Dead Sea Scrolls at the monastery of Qumran.[1] These groups were the result of experiences in the Jewish past and stood for different ways of interpreting the Jewish heritage.

---

[1]The Dead Sea Scrolls are a collection of biblical and other writings, written in the period before and after Jesus' birth, hidden when the monastery at Qumran, near the Dead Sea, was abandoned in AD 68, and not found until 1947 – 56.

Other Christians were Greeks, by race or by culture. Greek ways (architecture, education, leisure activities, and, above all, language) had come to pervade the lands of the Mediterranean seaboard, especially in the eastern half. Palestine itself, the homeland of Judaism, was far from being exempt from their influence, strong and distinctive though Jewish culture was. Even nationalist and assertive Jews were content to use the Greek language, as finds at Qumran and elsewhere have shown (see G. Vermes, *The Dead Sea Scrolls in English,* Penguin, 1975).

So Christians differed from the start in the way they felt and expressed their faith, because of their different backgrounds. All through our study of the beliefs of the first Christians, we need to remember both the fact that they held essentially one faith and the fact that they looked at it through different eyes.

Let us turn now to some of the beliefs which they brought with them as they turned to Christianity. To begin at the most general points, all of them, whether Jewish or Greek in background, would have shared certain broad beliefs about the universe, beliefs so different from those we take for granted that they need to be explicitly brought to our notice. We might say that they had a strongly religious view of the universe, in the sense that they took for granted the power and importance of spiritual forces of many kinds—angels, demons, deities, spirits, as well as the supreme God himself. The titles of these beings, the powers attributed to various elements among them, and especially the way in which the supreme God was regarded, varied greatly; and Jews above all would have been horrified to be lumped together with the rest. Still, they shared with others this strong sense of the spiritual world and its role in the affairs of earthly life. You only have to read the book of Daniel in the Old Testament, or the Qumran War Rule (see G. Vermes, *The Dead Sea Scrolls in English,* pp.122ff.) to see how vivid this could be, while the Revelation to John in the New Testament illustrates the same point from an early Christian setting.

Christians of varied background also shared their sense of the size and proportions of the universe. By comparison with our picture of the immensity of space, with earth as a mere speck, they saw it as small and compact, with the earth as its centre, even though, as we have seen, it was under the power and influence of spiritual forces outside it, some of them working through the visible stars.

This whole aspect of belief was a matter of intense interest to many at the time when Christianity began. The world hummed with ideas about it: the details of the spiritual beings, their number and their titles, the powers exerted by them through the stars, and above all, the hopes and fears they inspired as a result of the control they were believed to possess over earthly events and fortunes. For many, it was a picture full of mystery and anxiety, and all the more alluring for that.

But the Jews, from whom many of the earliest Christians came, and perhaps all those who wrote works which survived to be part of the New Testament, had certain strong beliefs of their own. What were they?

Above all, whatever importance they gave to angels or devils, they were convinced of the overwhelming power and reality of the one God of the whole world. He was awesome beyond belief—so *holy* indeed (to use the technical word for this quality of his) that his name, Yahweh, must not be uttered. While he was indeed creator and ruler of the whole world, nevertheless his relationship with the Jewish people was unique. It went back to the foundation of their life in the call of Abraham (Gen. 17:1 – 8). They were his chosen ones, recipients of his favour, but they were also his servants, with a message for all mankind about his power as their creator, ruler and judge.

7

The relationship was rooted in the Jewish story: the long tale, told in their scriptures (the Old Testament of the Christians), eventful and tumultuous, yet coming to rest time and again in God's faithful love for his people and his call for their allegiance. His rescue of them from slavery in Egypt centuries before (the event called the Exodus and described in ancient saga in the book of that name) made a picture, never to be forgotten, of his relationship with them. Whatever happened, however great the strains on their link with God, this was at the heart of their religion. They recalled it constantly in their worship and their festivals, above all in the Passover.

Jews traced to the time of the Exodus their greatest tangible gift fom God: the Law, given through their leader Moses. The Law, recorded in the first five books of the Old Testament, was the foundation of their life and faith. It brought them God's will—the way in which they could serve him perfectly, in every detail of life. Its study occupied the attention of all serious Jews, with a view to their applying it in every new situation in life. To get a sense of their devotion to the Law, read with care Psalm 119. To the casual reader, or someone without sympathy for any such approach to life, it often seems drearily repetitive. But enter into it, try and feel the loving concentration of life which it expesses in line after line. Though Jews disagreed about many aspects of the Law's meaning, it was for all of them the supreme gift, the unrivalled guide. To be outside the Law was to be no Jew. It was the centre of true faith, the sure path to the knowledge of God.

But the Law not only provided guidance for the Jews in the present, it had deep roots in the past. In that way, their faith had a strong historical sense. The other side of that sense was their hope and conviction about the future. If God was faithful to his promises for his people, then he *must* intervene to put right their wretched condition, scattered as they were all over the known world and oppressed by foreign powers in their own land. But if God is to intervene, then it must be by an act of extraordinary and immense power, mustering all his spiritual forces, and it must be decisive for the whole world. He will judge and rule. No one will any more be able to ignore his claims or doubt his justice. The creator of all things will have asserted his undoubted rights. It will be a time of catastrophe, yet also of marvellous joy for God's faithful ones. Such a hope absorbed the imagination and fervent hope of many Jews at this time.

Equipped with these beliefs, in various forms and with different emphases, people became Christians and turned to new beliefs. And if one thing is more and more clear it is this: that in one way or another, by one route or another, it was Jesus who made the decisive difference. However his influence came to be felt by this individual or that, this group or that, he it is who is responsible for the change in their beliefs. He was the new ingredient which made all the difference, the feature which transformed the picture of their beliefs. Yet he did not obliterate what they believed before. The old beliefs are visible in the forms of the new, and while transformation is a good word to describe them all, its degree naturally varied from one belief to another. The early Christians' own word for what had happened, *fulfilment,* perhaps hits it off as well as any.

So then, who was Jesus? And what did the first Christians believe about him? Before we answer these quesions and so embark on our first main topic, we must pause to ask, *how do we know about these matters at all?*

The New Testament

We know about Jesus and the first Christians from the writings which those Christians left behind them. Almost certainly all of them were written within a hundred years of the ministry of Jesus, and many, including the letters of Paul,

9

within forty years. We look at them now as *writings;* but immediately behind all of them stand *communities,* that is, groups of Christians from whose life they sprang and whose needs they met. They are much closer to life than most books written today, in the relative isolation of a scholar's study or a novelist's country cottage. So it is important to get the feel of them as far more than simply words on a page, and to let them bring to life again those who produced them. Each of them, in effect, shows us what some early Christian and those around him believed. It admits us to their thoughts and circumstances, shows what dangers and problems beset them, how they grasped new opportunities and worked out answers to new questions. In that way, these are very practical books.

Look at Paul's first letter to the Corinthians, for example. We see him dealing in turn with a whole battery of difficulties. Should Christians marry or not, in view of their belief that the end of the world was near (ch. 7)? Should they feel free to eat meat blessed at pagan temples (chs. 8 and 10)? What about their own worship, when preachers became lost in ecstasy and could no longer be understood (ch. 14), or when the congregation fell apart into separate groups (ch. 11) and loyalties (ch. 1)? In each case, we can see Paul bringing his beliefs to bear on the problem, often with difficulty and pain.

Each writing reflects its own situation and its own writer's way of believing. Each has his own favourite words. In his letter to the Romans, Paul is continually talking about the necessity of *faith* as the key attitude to God. By it he means a simple, trusting openness, which is the very opposite of all attemps to commend oneself to God by being virtuous. John however repeats time and again that *love* is the great mark of Christians and the bond between them and God.

But different emphases do not mean that each is simply going his own way, believing what he likes. Both are already aware of belonging to the Christian tradition. Paul, giving a summary of his belief, is careful to tell that he inherited it and did not invent it. It has an authority wider than his own, 'For I delivered to you as of first importance what I also received, that Christ died for our sins in accordance with the scriptures . . .' (1 Cor. 15:3). And John stresses that his belief goes back to 'the beginning', to roots in Jesus (1 John 1:1 – 4).

All this is most obviously true of the letters which make up the greater number of items in the New Testment. Is it true also of the gospels and the Acts of the Apostles? After all, they look like straightforward biographies or history-books. So in a way they are. They tell the story of Jesus' life, death and resurrection, and of how the church grew in its first twenty years. But they were not written in universities, with the aims and resources of modern research. They too sprang from the life of Christian congregations, intent upon living out and finding words for their new faith. They too reflect the needs and problems of those congregations. They too express various ways of believing, as well as unity of commitment to Jesus.

Three of the gospel writers (Matthew, Mark and Luke) used each other's books, in some order or other. The facts are these: all three share a great deal of material, including most of Mark, the shortest of the three; and Matthew and Luke share some material not in Mark. Most probably, Mark wrote his book first and this was used as a basis by the other two. Then they either drew upon another source (now lost) or else one used the other (probably Luke used Matthew). This is important because we can often lay three (or two) versions of the same story side by side and make our comparison. Try for example looking at the first eleven verses of Mark's Gospel alongside Matthew 3 and Luke 3. All the facts referred to above can be seen there: much material common to all three accounts, and some shared by only Matthew and Luke. Yet each puts the story in his own way and in his own setting. To ponder these passages is to get the situation in a nutshell. (See Brian E. Beck, *Reading the New Testament Today*, Lutterworth 1977, and T. G. A. Baker, *What is the New Testament?*, S.C.M. Press 1968.)

3
What did they believe about Jesus?

We said in the last chapter (p. 9) that in one way or another, and by one route or another, it was Jesus who made the decisive difference to the New Testament writers. Their previous beliefs varied in shape, content and emphasis, but to all of them Jesus brought, to a greater or lesser degree, transformation. So we need to grasp both the fact of the transformation and the variety of forms which it took. We must not expect the writers (and so, presumably, the congregations to which they belonged) to see Jesus in exactly the same way. They honour him by different means. They use different words and ideas. Yet their ways of honouring him fall into two categories. We shall consider these and then draw the threads together.

The one sent by God
A common feature of societies which are conscious of some deep need is for them to look for a deliverer. Depending on the kind of society and the form of its need, he may take a religious or political colouring. Often both aspects will be present. We may think of islanders in the South Seas, with their hope of a great visitor who will bring prosperity; or of Germany in the early thirties, poised to welcome Hitler.

The fact that this kind of hope is called 'messianism' points us straight back to Palestine in the first century. Among some of the Jews, there was a hope for the appearance of a 'messiah' (Hebrew for 'anointed one', a title which referred to the ceremony designating kings; in Greek, *christos*). The hope was that he would restore their national fortunes, free them from Roman occupation and establish God's rule on earth.

This expectation took various forms. The figure might be a new king of the stature and family of David, the great king of a thousand years before. He might share his role with a priestly leader. His coming might be part and parcel of the divine drama which would establish a whole new world-order of even, in some sense, bring the ordinary course of history to an end (see ch. 7). Or it might be more soberly political in character. Bar Cochba, who led the final revolt of the Jews in Palestine against the Romans in the 130s, was just such a liberator messiah and was thought of in those terms.

So, even within the relatively narrow sphere of first century Judaism, such hope can take many forms. All depends on the case. It depends on the one who arouses or fulfils it—the one who is sent—and on the people who respond. In the case of Jesus, then, it is not as if there was a fixed pattern to which he had to conform. Rather, there was a range of possibilities within which he could make his own way. He could put his own stamp upon the role and play it as he chose. In his hands, and in the hands of those who gave it to him, the title, messiah or christ, would take its own special colouring. Not *any* christ, but *Jesus* Christ.

Still, 'Christ'did carry the basic feeling of divine mission, and in belief about Jesus that was fundamental. He was the one sent by God. In Christian reflection on Jesus, we find that idea as early as Paul, writing about AD 50, 'When the time had fully come, God sent forth his Son' (Gal. 4:4). And it is one of the key ideas of the later Gospel of John, in which words for 'send' occur on almost every page. 'For God sent the Son into the world, not to condemn the world, but that the world might be saved through him' (John 3:17).

As these passages show, 'Christ' is closely linked to the title 'son' or 'son of God'. Again, this was a way of understanding him, dating from as far back as we can go. Paul uses this title a number of times, apart from the passage just quoted. It is at the heart of the story of Jesus' baptism, placed prominently at the start of the oldest gospel, 'And a voice came from heaven, "Thou art my beloved Son; with thee I am well pleased"' (Mark 1:11). It appears most extensively of all in the Gospel of John, and it was put in beautiful, full-dress story form in the tale of Jesus' birth told in Luke 1-2. No doubt it is now impossible to uncover the layer of history beneath this story. It is a kind of saga which shows the wonder of Jesus as God's son.

This title came to Jesus along lines exactly like those taken by the title 'messiah', with which indeed it was linked in its history and associations. But, like messiah and to a greater degree, it was a title with many applications. Angels, kings of Israel, faithful believers, the people of Israel as a whole, all these could be called 'sons of God'. As with messiah, the title receives special definition and sharp focus in being applied to Jesus. As the one sent by God, *he* is *the* Son.

It is worth breaking off to consider more closely this giving of titles to Jesus. These terms have become part of Christian vocabulary and we are used to them, but they represent a way of expressing belief which is not entirely plain. It is not one which we nowadays should naturally adopt if we were starting from scratch.

Think of three ways in which we apply titles in our society. First, as an honour (e.g. the Duke of Plaza Toro, Sir John Snooks); second, as an office (e.g. the Lord Mayor, the Bishop of London); third, as a kind of nickname given to someone we have come to appreciate (e.g. a tennis player might be called the queen of Wimbledon or a popular girl in a garrison town, at any rate in comic opera, the darling of the regiment). To which of these three categories do the titles of Jesus, in their original application, most aptly belong? Surely not quite the first or the second. Jesus was not at first called 'messiah' or 'son of God' as an honour, giving him status; nor does either of them signify a recognised office which he was plainly seen to occupy. It is true that as time went on their use in relation to him took on something of both these senses, but in origin they were much more like the third category. This was partly because, as we have seen, the titles were themselves not particularly clear-cut in their meaning, but it was also because people as they responded to his work, his teaching and his character found the titles drawn out of them as appropriate ways of appreciating Jesus. Approximate as they were, they fitted sufficiently well, and he filled both with new and specific content, simply by the power of the conviction which he created, that he was the one sent by God.

Instead of using such titles as these, our tendency today is to describe the functions performed by the person we have in mind. Indeed, this is the kind of language I have been using in giving an account of their meaning. We think in terms of what Jesus did or what role he performed. The first Christians, by contrast, took these convictions out of the realm of ideas and made them into labels or slogans which they then attached to Jesus' person. Not so much 'he *did* God's work' as 'he *was* God's son'. We could say that the titles reflected the ideas and put them in a vivid form.

The comprehensive one

In the time of Jesus, honoured figures had titles heaped upon them, whether they fitted together logically or not. The greater the honour, the wider the range of titles. It was particularly true of the Roman Emperor—and is still true of modern monarchs. The extent of the honour was determined by the impact made by the person concerned. As a reading of John 1:35 – 51 conveniently shows, Jesus received many such titles. They include, Lamb of God, messiah, Son of God, king of Israel, and Son of Man.

So great was his impression upon his followers that they quickly saw his significance on the widest possible scale. It may seem strange to us, but once we grasp the transforming effect of his mission, we can see why some Jewish Christians soon attributed to Jesus a role which stretched right from the beginning of all things to their end. Just as earlier titles we examined reflected the inner experience and conviction of those who believed, so other terms reflected the total quality of his importance for them.

Thus, as early as Paul, and perhaps even before he was writing his letters in the fifties, some Christians took old Jewish pictures of God's way of creating the world and adapted them to give Jesus the key place. The old pictures began from the idea that the world manifested order and planning. So, they had said, it bore clear signs of God's wisdom and of his power of command. He had, we might say, thought it out and spoken his will. This idea was put in pictorial form. At the creation, God had 'wisdom', seen almost as a female consort, by his side; or else, he used his 'word' as a kind of servant. Belief in angels as God's court made such picturing natural. This passage from Proverbs 8.27 – 30, in which Wisdom is speaking, illustrates the point vividly,

When he established the heavens, I was there...
when he marked out the foundations of the earth,
then I was beside him, like a master workman;
and I was daily his delight, rejoicing before him always.

As Jesus was thought of as sent by God as his messenger, it is not difficult to see how he could be regarded as the embodiment of God's wisdom and God's word. If he was indeed God's chosen one, then was he not the one who had been God's agent in creation? This development was aided by the fact that Jews already attributed such 'pre-existence' (to give it its technical name) to the Law, the heart of *their* way of seeing contact between God and the world.

We can see the result in a reference by Paul to 'Jesus Christ, through whom are all things and through whom we exist' (1 Cor: 8.6), and, most clearly of all, in the opening of the Gospel of John,

> In the beginning was the Word, and the Word was with God, and the Word was God. He was in the beginning with God; all things were made through him, and without him was not anything made that was made.

Similarly, if Jesus was the one sent by God, then the winding up of the world would take place through him, with all the events expected on that great and awesome day, in particular the resurrection of the dead for judgement and the establishing of God's clear rule over the whole world by the defeat of all opposing powers.

Christians had Jewish ideas ready to hand (see p. 9). In the book of Daniel (7:13), there is a reference to 'one like a son of man' (which means 'a figure in human form'), who is involved in these events as God's great agent, and who is given power over the whole world. So Jesus was seen as '*the* son of man'. He was none other than the central figure in this drama which would round off history and show without a shadow of doubt God's true position in relation to the world.

We see Jesus stepping into this role in passages like these from the Gospel of Mark,

> For whoever is ashamed of me and of my words in this adulterous and sinful generation, of him will the Son of man also be ashamed, when he comes in the glory of his Father with the holy angels (8.38).

> And then they will see the Son of man coming in clouds with great power and glory. And then he will send out the angels, and gather his elect from the four winds, from the ends of the earth to the ends of heaven (13:26).

Whatever we may make of statements like these, there is no mistaking the atmosphere of foreboding and almost of terror to which they testify.

In fact this title, 'Son of man', is much the commonest given to Jesus in the gospels. Originally, it may have been taken by him or given to him in a more straightforward and ordinary sense. For among Jews of the time of Jesus, it seems to have been an expression by which a man might refer to himself modestly and self-effacingly, much as some English people say 'one' when they mean 'I'. But clearly, it was soon seen in the light of the passage in Daniel, with its reference to one in human form ('one like a son of man'), and given its much more full-blooded sense with its mind-boggling implications. We may have an example of the less technical sense in a saying like this,

Foxes have holes, and birds of the air have nests; but the Son of man has nowhere to lay his head (Matt: 8.20).

The sense of the comprehensiveness of Jesus reaches its climax in passages like John 1:1 and 20:28, where Thomas addresses him as no less than 'My Lord and my God'. Jesus *represents* God to us. No statement lower than this could do justice to the all-embracing nature of his work and its effects as Christians knew them.

Our account has concentrated on two aspects of belief about Jesus and will seem to have neglected some of the most important sides of it. What about his death and his resurrection? What about his moral teaching? These and other sides of the matter will figure in later chapters. But this much may be said now. By the time even the earliest parts of the New Testament were written (that is, in the earliest and only evidence open to us), Jesus was not only one whom Christians had beliefs *about,* he was the one they believed *in.*

They saw him as then and there involved with them, close, present, alive. This they attributed to his resurrection. The living Jesus was the strong agent by means of whom God had intervened and still intervened for man's salvation.

4
What did they believe about God?

You may think that this chapter should have preceded the last, and from one point of view you would be right. Both logically and historically, belief about God comes before belief about Jesus. But if we are trying to capture in words the belief of the first Christians, then the chapter on Jesus has every right to pride of place. For them, he occupied the centre of the stage. He had kindled their imaginations afresh, and restructured the whole pattern of their faith, so much so that there is a sense in which, in the New Testament, God remains in the background.

This often results in books about the thought of the New Testament paying hardly any attention to this topic. The impression is given that the new Christian faith simply built on settled Jewish foundations, taking beliefs about God for granted and giving its main attention to other subjects, above all Jesus and the new life assured by him.

In one sense, this is not unfair. Chistians had no thought at all of believing in a different God from the Jews, however fresh and new they felt their faith to be. The first article of the Apostles' Creed (with origins going back to the second century) is 'I believe in God the Father almighty, maker of heaven and earth'. This is a perfectly fair summary of early Christian belief in God, and no Jew would have dissented from it.

When in the second century a teacher called Marcion arose, who did not hold that the Christians' God was one and the same as that of the Jews, it is true that he won a substantial following, but the mainstream church had no hesitation in rejecting him. On the contrary, the Christians' claim was precisely that their faith fulfilled the faith of Israel and God's age-old promises to his people. The opening of the letter to the Hebrews expresses it succinctly,

> In many and various ways God spoke of old to our fathers by the prophets; but in these last days he has spoken to us by a Son, whom he appointed the heir of all things (Heb. 1:1 – 2).

Many Christians put a great deal of effort into showing how the career of Jesus had been prophesied both in general and in detail by the Jewish scriptures, the Old Testament. They found it was important to be able to show this, both for themselves, in that the one God had now brought his purpose to its climax, and for their discussions with Jews, who denied their claims.

Matthew's Gospel, for example, is punctuated frequently with quotations from the Old Testament, which the writer sees as bearing directly on Jesus and indeed as having been written for that very purpose. In particular, the first two chapters of the book are almost wholly written on that basis. So, while a modern student of Hosea (11:1) reads the words, 'Out of Egypt have I called my son', as referring to the Exodus under Moses centuries before, Matthew (2:15) has no difficulty in stating that it was written to be fulfilled in the incident from Jesus' infancy which he describes.

Underlying this treatment of the Old Testament is the conviction that the God *of Israel* has sent his Son, with a message of salvation for *all men*. Matthew rounds off his book, looking out towards the mission of the church with the words, 'Go therefore and make disiciples of all nations' (28:19).

Nevertheless, it is true of belief in God as of all other beliefs held by the first Christians that Jesus had somehow transformed it. It is not enough to say that the new faith built upon settled foundations, if that is taken to mean that it left them unaffected. As a result of Jesus, belief in God itself received new colouring. It came to be held with distinctive emphases.

What exactly were these emphases and how much weight should we place on them? At this point, there is room for disagreement. This is partly because the first Christians themselves differed in the way in which, and the degree to which, their original Jewish faith was transformed. It is not easy to get a clear overall picture. But other factors also affect the matter.

It is in the nature of converts to a new faith to exaggerate the extent of its difference from what they previously held, and even to disparage their old faith unfairly. So, from reading Paul, particularly in the letters to the Galatians and Romans, Christians have built up a picture of the Judaism of his time as wholly based on the attempt to win God's approval by obedience to his commands. By contrast, God had now offered man acceptance and forgiveness by an act of sheer, free generosity in Christ. The old way was characterised by law, with its inevitable accompaniments of striving, failure, and guilt, and the new by grace, with its assurance of a gift received and of welcome to those who turn and trust God. The last words of Romans 5 give a typical impression,

> Law came in, to increase the trespass; but where sin increased, grace abounded all the more, so that, as sin reigned in death, grace also might reign through righteousness to eternal life through Jesus Christ our Lord (Rom. 5:20 – 21).

It seems, however, that most reflective Jews at the time of Paul would have failed to recognise their faith in this account. For them, Judaism was equally a way of life given by God's gift, an open and generous way, not guilt-ridden at all, but marked by ready forgiveness and willing love. And the Law, far from being a tyrant and a frustration, was a gracious provision to enable man to tread his way happily and obediently through the world.

Other early Christians were less deeply affected by the newness of the life made available as a result of Jesus. The letter of James, for example, displays an outlook well within the ways of traditional piety. Matthew presents Jesus teaching his followers to adhere to the full Jewish Law (5:17 – 19; 23:23)—they are not to neglect even the details of the Law—while infusing into it a spirit of strenuous attention to inner motive (see the contrasts in 5:21 – 48) and giving priority to the command to love (22:34 – 40). Probably Jewish teachers would have contested little of this, and indeed Matthew reserves his condemnation for the performance rather than the teaching of the scribes and Pharisees (see ch. 23, especially v. 3).

But to whatever degree Christians allowed their faith to transform their previous convictions about God and his ways with man, all united in seeing Jesus as God's agent and his coming as the climax to which everything before it had led. Even Matthew, whose presentation of Jesus' *teaching* arguably shows him to differ little from the Jewish rabbis, gives a *total* picture of him which makes his coming crucial and decisive. This puts the way of life taught by him in a wholly new light, for it is lived in his gracious presence. 'Where two or three are gathered in my name, there am I in the midst of them' (18:20). Thus, for all of them, God himself is now ' the God and Father of our Lord Jesus Christ', as 1 Peter 1:3 puts it. The reader must decide how much difference it makes that God is now seen as the one who 'so loved the world that he gave his only Son, that whoever believes in him should not perish but have eternal life' (John 3:16). Is this not a God with a newly vivid human face, a God whose personal quality is focused with new sharpness, who has somehow stepped forward on to the human stage?

To read the Gospels of Matthew, Mark and Luke is like looking at one of those drawings in children's books which are two pictures in one. For example, you might see either a rabbit with its ears hanging down or an old gentleman wearing a cravat; or else, either a shapely goblet or two faces looking at each other. What are you to say the Gospels are about? How are you to sum up their subject in a word? About Jesus, you may say without hesitation. But look again. Is not Jesus on every page pushing your attention elsewhere? Near the beginning of his book, the first account of Jesus to be written, Mark summarised his mission and message thus,

The time is fulfilled, and the kingdom of God is at hand; repent and believe in the gospel (1:15).

Jesus' whole subject is 'the kingdom of God'. Are not Jesus' parables further clear evidence? A glance at Matthew 13, which is a collection of these parables, shows the expression, 'the kingdom', occurring no less than a dozen times. All these stories aim to show the value or the importance of the kingdom. Moreover, it is almost certainly right to see Jesus' acts of power as intended to make exactly the same point, 'the kingdom of God has drawn near'.

To see this, you have only to read Isaiah 35:2 – 6,

They shall see the glory of the Lord,
    the majesty of our God . . .
Then the eyes of the blind shall be opened,
    and the ears of the deaf unstopped;
then shall the lame man leap like a hart,
    and the tongue of the dumb sing for joy.

It is a picture of the wonderful new world God would one day bring, the object of his people's longing. Does it not read almost like a programme for the Jesus we read about in the gospels?

Some modern writers (see recently Don Cupitt, *Jesus and the Gospel of God*, Lutterworth, 1979, and, with Peter Armstrong, *Who was Jesus?* B.B.C.,1977) hold that Jesus was neither more nor less than a supremely powerful and compelling spokesman for God. He proclaimed the simple but, if you take it seriously, overwhelming fact of the reality of God. God, immediate, close, gracious, loving, urgently demanding all allegiance: God sovereign over all men and all things. That was the message of Jesus, and this is what the phrase 'the *kingdom* of God' signifies. Understandably but regrettably, these writers claim, early Christians quickly moved away from the memory of this message. So struck were they by Jesus the messenger that they turned their attention from Jesus' message to Jesus himself and made him more and more the object of their allegiance and devotion. So, while Jesus pointed to God, Christians soon came to point instead to Jesus.

On this reading of the situation, the first three gospels, which may be seen as closer to the actual teaching and work of Jesus than the Gospel of John, reflect both stages of the process, both Jesus as he really was and Jesus as the church came to see him, the Jesus of history and the Jesus of faith.

But does this shift represent quite such an obvious distortion as this account suggests? Certainly, it is a distortion in so far as it distracts us from the power of Jesus' message. Because the expression, 'the kingdom of God', plays such a small part in Jewish thought at the time (as far as our not very abundant evidence goes) and yet is so prominent in the first three gospels, it looks as if it represents truly the orginal emphasis of Jesus and accurately conveys to us a sense of his prophetic concentration and single-mindedness. We fail to hear Jesus if we fail to grasp this teaching in all its searching power and in its ability to confront us starkly with the living and inescapable God.

It is also a distortion in so far as it opened the door to a devotion to Jesus which has often gone its own peculiar way and turned him into an image of all kinds of human aspirations, plausible and implausible. History has given us the imperial Jesus and the liberator Jesus, the English Jesus and the African Jesus, all owing more to the imagination of believers than to the figure of first century Palestine.

But it was both inevitable and no distortion when, in their great gratitude, Christians came to see in Jesus one who in his own person expressed and embodied the message of his life. If God's rule was to be experienced anywhere, it was where Jesus was. His death and resurrection gave the greatest possible stimulus to this process. He was indeed the agent of God's rule.

The error, then, was to give the impression that Jesus was in any way independent of the God to whose reality he had faithfully testified in life and death. Sometimes the New Testament, in its exuberant concentration on Jesus, can be taken to convey such a sense. But that is to misread it. He was God's agent, and, equally and conversely, it was God whose agent he was.

5
What did they believe about themselves?

Why do people take up a new belief? Particularly in its early days, it is often not because it convinces bystanders by the force of its argument. It is more because it meets strongly felt needs. (We may think of the rise of National Socialism in Germany in the 1930s.) Of course those needs themselves will in the process come to be felt with new clarity, especially in the case of a faith as dynamic as the early Christian message; but still, the needs are there first, waiting to be satisfied.

What then were the needs which people felt at the time of Jesus, and which soon attracted them in considerable numbers to the faith which sprang from him?

The most general term for the object of widespread human longing at this time was *salvation*. With us, this is almost exclusively a religious term, and religion has become for many an area of specialised interest. At the time we are concerned with, what we should call the religious dimension was much more part of the ordinary structure of life, and so, in a sense, more prosaic, more taken for granted. So the word *security* may give a more graphic impression of what people were after. In one way or another, depending on what threats they felt, people wanted to be *safe*.

It was therefore a wide-ranging need and could take a great variety of forms. It covered the sort of security the Roman Emperor might be expected to provide, that is, from barbarians across the frontiers and anarchy within the Empire. It covered too security beyond death, or in the face of life's many hazards, which was to be sought in the cults which abounded at this time, especially in the eastern Mediterranean lands. It included the hope of security from the spiritual powers which were seen, in the pre-scientific age, as responsible for many of the ills of life. And we should not forget how much more immediately pressing many of those ills were when there was little understanding of disease and hardly any cushioning against famine and natural disaster. No wonder it has been called an 'age of anxiety'.

For some, this longing for security included a strong desire for sheer knowledge of the spiritual world and the plan of history. If only one knew about that, then indeed one could feel secure. For many, it all amounted to a plain longing to escape.

Put in these ways, much of it seems to us hardly a religious aspiration at all. It is when we turn to the Jewish sphere that we feel on more familiar ground. There a more moral note is struck. What people felt they needed was not simply to 'know', or to be protected against the dangers of a frightening world, but also to be on a right footing with God. How can we please God, do right by him? How can we overcome our deep-seated tendency to fail him, to sin against him, to disobey his known will? If only we could win that fight, then indeed we should be secure.

More precisely still, for the Jew real security was that which God would finally assure on the last day, when he would intervene to wind up the present order of the world. In technical language, 'salvation' was a strongly eschatological (from Greek *eschatos* meaning 'last') concept.

In societies where people felt these needs keenly, the Christian faith indeed took root. It follows that they found in it the way to meet them. People turned to Jesus and to the faith which stemmed from him because they found in him the means of satisfying—and often indeed the means of identifying—their deepest needs.

It is not surprising that, as they varied in their needs, so the accounts they gave of Jesus' work to meet them also differed. In the New Testament, we find a number of ways of describing his effect upon his followers and upon the world. We can put them all under the umbrella of 'salvation', or we might say that for everybody who turned to him, he made, as we put it, 'all the difference'. He revolutionised their outlook, their hopes, and their possibilities. Let us take examples.

Undoubtedly, many early Christians were aware of a new confidence in face of the hazards of life, including death itself. Jesus, they said, had overcome the spiritual powers, and his followers could walk secure. His victory had taken place on the small scale during his life-time, in the exorcisms and healings he had performed, and on the universal scale, in his death and resurrection.

Further, those who believed in him had in baptism (see p. 53) the means of entering into those events and so sharing his victory. 'Do you not know that all of us who have been baptized into Christ Jesus were baptized into his death? We were buried therefore with him by baptism into death, so that as Christ was raised from the dead by the glory of the Father, we too might walk in newness of life.' Such is Paul's strong, vivid imagery and doctrine (Rom. 6:3 – 4).

Clearly, this did not mean that Christians had received charmed lives. Suffering and death still overtook them, indeed were willingly accepted. What then did their conviction mean in practical terms? We get the clearest answer to this question from Paul in Romans 8:35 – 39.

Who shall separate us from the love of Christ? Shall tribulation, or distress, or persecution, or famine, or nakedness, or peril, or sword?... No, in all these things we are more than conquerors through him who loved us. For I am sure that neither death, nor life, nor angels, nor principalities, nor things present, nor things to come, nor powers, nor height, nor depth, nor anything else in all creation, will be able to separate us from the love of God in Christ Jesus our Lord.

29

The last words are the key. As far as Paul was concerned, none of the ills that face us ('principalities' and 'powers' are terms for the spiritual forces believed to be responsible for them) can invalidate or count against God's love for us, now that it has been made plain in Christ. Whatever the appearances, that is secure. There we see the measure and the strong thrust of Paul's faith.

The first Christians were also aware of forgiveness of their sins. This was more than a distant act of bounty. They felt that they had been brought into a completely new sphere of existence, with their relationship with God now set on a fresh foundation. They had been accepted and given a new start, surrounded by his gracious favour. Again, there was no question of magical immunity from sin. Moral life remained a serious business, full of pitfalls. Indeed, a new sense of the pervasiveness and insidiousness of sin accompanied the new sense of release. 'All have sinned and fall short of the glory of God,' wrote Paul (Rom. 3:23). There was, however, now a new security and also a new hope.

Paul's leading term for the new acceptance which God has given is 'justification' (which in Greek is of the same family of words as those which we usually translate as 'righteous', 'righteousness'). Consider this statement, a summary of Paul's teaching, 'Since we are justified by faith, we have peace with God through our Lord Jesus Christ. Through him we have obtained access to this grace in which we stand, and we rejoice in our hope of sharing the glory of God' (Rom. 5:1 – 2).

Judaism often pictured the relationship between God and man as a kind of debate or disputation, and in describing it drew upon the language of the law-court where such activity was most familiar. The use of this imagery ensured that the essential moral aspect was present. So Paul is expressing his new Christian confidence by saying that it is as if God has given us the status of persons acquitted, something which we had no business to expect. It is an act of sheer generosity, to which man has only to respond in pure trust.

If we are to understand Paul, we must dig beneath this language and recapture the sense of exhilaration and assurance which it expresses. It is a great wonder that God has acted thus. It is sheer grace. The New Testament presents us with two opposite difficulties in doing this digging and recapturing. On the one hand, it comes from a culture alien to us, and unless we are aware of that, we are either puzzled by its words or miss their full meaning. On the other hand, it comes to us overlaid by centuries of familiar Christian use, much of it lacking close attention to the writers' original sense. Both serve to blur the picture for us. Nowhere is this more true than with Paul. With no New Testament writer is it more necessary to insist on trying to enter into the underlying experience which his words express.

Not only did he feel new freedom and assurance. He felt also a new sense of reconciliation with God. 'God was in Christ reconciling the world to himself, not counting their trespasses against them, and entrusting to us the message of reconciliation' (2 Cor. 5:19). In his Jewish world, animal sacrifices, offered in the temple at Jerusalem, were the ritual means by which a sinner sought to claim forgiveness and reestablish his friendship with God. So Paul, convinced that this friendship had been given decisively through Jesus, naturally saw him in sacrificial terms. So he was led to concentrate on Jesus' death and to say little about his actual life. Because of Paul's way of understanding the effects of Jesus, it was his death and resurrection which above all commanded his attention. Jesus' death, then, was for Paul the sacrifice offered to God to bring about our reconciliation to God, our 'peace' (Rom. 5:1).

In relation to this theme, Paul was deeply influenced by the Old Testament story of Abraham's binding of his son Isaac for sacrifice (Gen: 22), a story much studied by Jewish teachers at this time. Some of them, developing the story as it stood, taught that Isaac had been a willing and obedient offering. This example of humble and total dedication was a perfect illustration for the role of Jesus. Paul quotes the old story in Romans 8:32, using language reminiscent of Genesis 22:16,

> *Paul:* He who did not spare his own Son but gave him up for us all...
> *Genesis:* Because ... you have not withheld your son, your only son, I will indeed bless you.

And he almost certainly has it in mind in Romans 3:25, 'Christ Jesus, whom God put forward as an expiation by his blood.' For Paul, the wonder of what had now occurred was that God himself had taken the initiative to bring about that new closeness to himself of which Paul was so deeply aware.

Like the Judaism from which they mostly came, the faith of the first Christians was chiefly concerned with two needs: to relate to God and to obey him. They became Christians because they found in the church a new and effective way of meeting those needs. They received a new status in relation to God, a new framework in which to serve him, and a new power to live according to his will. In their various ways, Jews and Greeks could welcome this overcoming of long-standing obstacles in their lives. They felt that the deepest human needs had been met and that, whatever their background, they had entered a new world. 'If any one is in Christ, there is a new creation' (2 Cor. 5:17).

The creative impulse behind this new self-awareness was Jesus. No wonder some of them spoke of him as a new Adam (the Hebrew word for 'man'). 'As in Adam all die, so also in Christ shall all be made alive' (1 Cor. 15:22). We have seen something of the imagery the first Christians used and the reasons they gave to explain how Jesus had brought about this belief concerning man's new situation and new hopes. No doubt the manner of his life and the content of his teaching had played the major part in giving rise to the belief. On the details of the chain of cause and effect, our sources are much less helpful than we, as historical enquirers, would wish. Using language which is often not immediately clear to us and which is sometimes frankly baffling, they place the weight on his death and resurrection; and it is not easy for us to see exactly how such events came to be seen to have these mighty effects. At root, though, however they put it, their belief was that God meant it to be so ('God raised him from the dead' (Rom. 10:9)). And their experience was certainly that it was so. Whether we find their *language* always helpful or not, at these two points we may be ready to meet them and share their conviction. (See John Knox, *The Death of Christ*, part III, Collins, 1959, and L. Grollenberg, *Paul*, S.C.M. Press, 1978.)

6
What did they believe
about their present?

It is all very well to know that you have a new and close relationship with God. But what do you then do? How do you look at life and map out your daily conduct? How do you regard the world around? We shall look in chapter 10 at the more detailed question of the views of the first Christians on right and wrong. Here we are interested in their more general attitude to life in the here and now.

As we have come to expect, they did not all go about answering these questions in the same way. Some did it in what we might consider the most straightforward manner. They looked back to the life and teaching of Jesus and set out to imitate and to obey. We know this from the very existence of the gospels, and especially two of them, those of Matthew and Luke. These are full of teaching of Jesus. They provide, each in its own way but with a good deal of common material, a vivid picture of Jesus and his teaching on many matters of practical concern.

This view is confirmed in the case of Matthew especially when we notice that his favourite word for a follower of Jesus is 'disciple'. But 'disciple' means 'pupil' or 'learner'. That is how Matthew sees a Christian's task. Look for example at the command of Jesus at the end of the book, 'Go therefore and make *disciples* of all nations' (Matt. 28:19). There is the church's permanent task outlined, and it is seen as enrolling pupils in the school of Jesus, God's chosen one.

Other Christians may have taken a somewhat similar view (that is, they saw Christian life as one of obedience to teaching), but looked elsewhere for their teacher when it was a question of the details of Christian living. The Pastoral Epistles (1 and 2 Timothy, and Titus) were probably written at the end of the first century or even a little later, that is, some forty years after the death of Paul to whose authorship they are ascribed. There are many reasons for thinking they are not by Paul himself, including the facts that they are very different in their approach and their contents from the letters we know Paul wrote, and use words unlike those used by Paul. The important thing for us to know is that writers in the ancient world saw nothing improper in putting a work under the name of another author, as it were to claim his authority and patronage. They were saying in effect, 'If he were now in our shoes, facing our problems, here is what he would say to you and here is what he would expect of you.'

The writer of the Pastoral Epistles sees the everyday arrangements of Christian life as following the teaching of Paul, as he himself was now adapting it and applying it to fresh circumstances. He gives to Jesus an exalted but somewhat formal place; he is the one who had been raised from the dead, is his people's saviour, and will return in power. The following sentence is typical of his way of combining moral concern with brief, doctrinal formulas about Jesus, 'I charge you to keep the commandment unstained and free from reproach until the appearing of our Lord Jesus Christ' (1 Tim. 6:14).

Paul looked at the whole matter differently. The key word for him is 'spirit'. This word has become a technical term in religion, used in a number of different ways. To understand the New Testament uses of it, it is best to put on one side any associations the word may have now acquired and go back to its roots. It comes from the Latin *spiritus,* whose original meaning is 'breath' or 'wind'; and behind the Bible's use of it, when it is applied to God's activity, lies the simple but vivid image of his work in the world resulting from his powerful breathing or blowing. A clear example is Psalm 104:30, 'When thou sendest forth thy Spirit, they are created; and thou renewest the face of the ground.'

By the time of Jesus the image had become somewhat formalised, but it still retained much of its power. Jews believed that at the coming great time when God would intervene to bring the world's present course to its end, there would be a great outpouring of his breath (or, if we wish to convey the word's increasingly technical sense, his spirit). It was a way of saying that God's immense power would then be unmistakable, and his purposes would be fully achieved. The prophet Joel had looked forward to this day,

> And it shall come to pass afterward,
>   that I will pour out my spirit on all flesh;
> your sons and your daughters shall prophesy,
>   your old men shall dream dreams,
>   and your young men shall see visions.
> Even upon the menservants and maidservants
>   in those days, I will pour out my spirit (Joel 2:28 – 29).

It is a clear sign of the strength of the first Christians' conviction that in Jesus and as a result of him God had begun his decisive intervention in the world, that they applied this very language to their own life. Luke, in writing Acts 2:17 – 21, quotes this passage from Joel in his account of the first Christian preaching shortly after the end of Jesus' earthly career, but even more strikingly, Paul sees Christian life as wholly directed and empowered by the Spirit. For him, what kept Christians alive and moving was not so much the teaching of Jesus, but that same power of God which had been active in him. 'If the Spirit of him who raised Jesus from the dead dwells in you, he who raised Christ Jesus from the dead will give life to your mortal bodies also through his Spirit which dwells in you' (Rom. 8:11).

He refers to Jesus' teaching and earthly career hardly at all. There is a reference to his teaching on divorce in

1 Corinthians 7:10 and an account of the Last Supper in 1 Corinthians 11:23 – 25, and, beyond that, very little. The whole life of the Christian churches which we read about in Paul's letters is dominated by this powerful force which they called the Spirit. In 1 Corinthians 14 we can see that sometimes it led to manifestations (especially the uttering of ecstatic and unintelligible sounds) of whose propriety Paul was uncertain. But there was no doubt of the strength of this power in the everyday life of Paul and the Christians who had learnt from him.

In other words, what mattered for these Christians was not so much the detailed following of a pattern of teaching, but rather a life directed by a new power from God. It was along these lines that Paul worked out the implications of what Christ had done. The effect on those who came to faith in him was existence at a new level. As the shorthand term for this new level was 'spirit', so the shorthand term for the old level was 'flesh'. When man is left to himself without the new awareness of the powerful driving-force from God, he lives on his own meagre resources and is full of his own self-centred concern. He lives at the level of the 'flesh'.

Each of the two levels has its own characteristics,

Now the works of the flesh are plain: immorality, impurity, licentiousness, idolatry, sorcery, enmity, strife, jealousy, anger, selfishness, dissension, party spirit, envy, drunkenness, carousing and the like... But the fruit of the Spirit is love, joy, peace, patience, kindness, goodness, faithfulness, gentleness, self-control (Gal. 5:19 – 21).

Notice that the contrast is not between what we might call bodily existence and spiritual life, but between two kinds of existence, each embracing the outward and inward life. Paul was not against the body!

Thirty or forty years later, the writer of the Gospel of John presented a more ordered picture along similar lines. He too saw Christian life as lived under the protection and guidance of the Spirit. He used a special word of his own which brings this out: Paraclete (from the Greek *parakletos*). 'I will pray the Father', says Jesus, 'and he will give you another Paraclete, to be with you for ever, even the Spirit of truth, whom the world connot receive' (John 14:16). We may translate this word 'counsellor' or 'defender'.

Despite this variety of approaches, all the writers we have looked at have this in common, that Jesus was the source of their present mode of life. Whether it is as model or as teacher or as the one whose spirit dwells among his people, he is the unseen presence. Matthew, who most strongly emphasised Jesus' role as teacher, ends his book, 'I am with you always.' And Paul wrote, 'It is no longer I who live, but Christ who lives in me; and the life I now live in the flesh I live by faith in the Son of God, who loved me and gave himself for me' (Gal. 2:20).

7
What did they believe about their future?

In writing about the first Christians' belief concerning the present, we did not refer to one crucial element. Unless it is speedily brought in, the picture will be misleading. That element is their belief about the future, a belief which affected, even dominated, their whole outlook. However strong their sense of what they had already received from God through Jesus and their confidence in God in the present, they looked forward to a future which would put even the marvellous present in the shade.

Though the urgency and power of this belief was less strong for some early Christians than for others, especially perhaps as the years went by, there were none for whom it was not of great significance. To feel what they felt, we have to make an effort of imagination.

Imagine you are watching a violent film; not a film picturing sadistic torture and cruelty, but rather a battle, with all its turmoil and confusion. As you watch, you are caught up in the noise and horror. You attach yourself to one side or the other. You could almost be there. Then the air clears. The leader of your side breaks through and victory is won. You are happy, relieved, safe.

That conveys something of the character of the future to which most of the early Christians looked forward. To see what sort of picture they had, read the following passages. The first is from what is perhaps Paul's earliest letter (and so the oldest Christian writing we have), dating from the early fifties; the second from teaching ascribed to Jesus in our oldest gospel, that of Mark, dating probably from about A.D. 70.

> We would not have you ignorant, brethren, concerning those who are asleep (i.e. have died), that you may not grieve as others do who have no hope...For this we declare to you by the word of the Lord, that we who are alive, who are left until the coming of the Lord, shall not precede those who have fallen asleep. For the Lord himself will descend from heaven with a cry of command, with the archangel's call, and with the sound of the trumpet of God. And the dead in Christ will rise first; then we who are alive, who are left, shall be caught up together with them in the clouds to meet the Lord in the air; and so we shall always be with the Lord (1 Thess. 4:13 – 17).

> When you hear of wars and rumours of wars, do not be alarmed; this must take place, but the end is not yet. For nation will rise against nation, and kingdom against kingdom; there will be earthquakes in various places, there will be famines; this is but the beginning of the sufferings...But in those days... the sun will be darkened, and the moon will not give its light, and the stars will be falling from heaven, and the powers in the heavens will be shaken. And then they will see the Son of man coming in clouds with great power and glory (Mark 13:7 – 8, 24 – 26).

The first Christians did not invent this kind of language. As we have seen (p. 9), they inherited it from Judaism, where too there was belief in a coming great intervention by God to judge the whole world and establish his rule. But as in everything else, the picture had been transformed, to one degree or another, as a result of Jesus.

It was not just that he was now seen as the central actor in the great drama (as the passages quoted illustrate). It was also that this future event was linked, because of Jesus, to what had already happened. He was not simply a figure of an imagined, mythical future, but a known and loved master who had only recently lived and taught in Galilee. And, as we have seen (p. 17), so impressive had his followers found him, that they felt that the conditions of the new world had already been set up among them. Where he had been at work, there

God's kingdom was already to be found, on the very threshold. Matthew and Luke both recorded a saying of Jesus, 'If it is by the Spirit of God that I cast out demons, then the kingdom of God has come upon you' (Matt. 12:28, Luke 11:20).

Similarly, the Christians talked of their own sense of God's power as the action of the Spirit, associated in everyday Jewish thought with the coming great days. And the resurrection of Jesus was a first instalment, a kind of trailer, foreshadowing and guaranteeing the future triumph of his chosen ones. Paul calls him the 'firstfruits' (1 Cor. 15:23), the first stage of a great harvest soon to be reaped.

In other words, even if the way they expressed their belief about the future may strike us as extravagant, strange, or lurid, at least it was all of a piece with something much easier to put your finger on, that is, the person and career of Jesus. That was God's powerful saving act, and the future was its extension on the grand scale, or, in their terms, its logical fulfilment. But the life of Jesus and the future to which they looked forward were seen as a single process. The belief in God's power to save lay behind both.

But we need to be clearer about their picture of the future. How exactly did they see it? The fullest account we have is in the Revelation to John. It is a Christian book, written on the model of Jewish books on the same subject, especially the book of Daniel and parts of the book of Ezekiel. To read it with concentration is like allowing yourself to be caught up in the war film to which we referred. You become part of a strange, mysterious, absorbing world first of anguish and then of joy and peace. It finishes with a vision of great beauty,

Then I saw a new heaven and a new earth; for the first heaven and the first earth had passed away, and the sea was no more. And I saw the holy city, new Jerusalem, coming down out of heaven from God, prepared as a bride adorned for her husband; and I heard a great voice from the throne saying, 'Behold, the dwelling of God is with men' (Rev. 21:1 – 3).

41

There the traditional Jewish element and the new figure of Christ meet. It is a new *Jerusalem,* and Christ is the husband awaited by his people.

Not all Christians looked to this future in exactly the same way, but it will be helpful to state the sort of programme many of them had in mind. Jesus, they believed, who had come as God's agent, now reigned in heaven. He had established in the world a band of followers, the church, among whom the results of his mission were still clearly to be seen. Soon, there would break out catastrophes of all kinds, especially wars and disturbances, in which the Christians would suffer persecution, as their master had done. But then all this would come to an end, for he would return to vindicate them and defeat those who were hostile to God's cause. The dead would be raised, all would be judged, and God's reign of love and peace would be finally established; and Jesus' great work as his agent would be accomplished. (For an early version of this, see 1 Corinthians 15:20 – 28.)

Two further aspects of this matter need to be discussed. First, though much of what is contained in the outline just given can be found in the writings of Paul, a similar picture is to be found in the gospels, for example in chapter 13 of Mark, which was quoted above. There it is depicted as part of the teaching of Jesus himself. Some of these accounts seem to reflect events known to have happened in the later years of the first century, some forty years after the time of Jesus. For example, the mysterious reference in Mark 13:14 to 'the desolating sacrilege' may well refer to the desecration of the temple in Jerusalem by the Romans in AD 70, and the mention of armies besieging the city in Luke 21:20 may reflect the same events.

What are we to make of these passages? Did Jesus in fact foresee these events, including the Jewish revolt against the Romans in AD 66 – 74, and see them as leading on to his own return in power (Mark 13:26)? Or have early Christians, regarding Jesus as, among other things, a great prophet, placed such teaching on his lips? Or have they filled out some of his teaching with further details, gathered from events that had occurred by the time they were writing? On these matters, there is room for a variety of views.

More important is the fact that these expectations were not fulfilled in the obvious sense. Time and events continued. History still goes on its way. How far was this fact already beginning to affect Christians in New Testament times, and what did they make of it?

Some seem simply to have pushed further into the future the end which they had once expected so soon. It is unlikely that many of them deferred it far into the future, but certainly they were able to accept such delay without undue disturbance. Already in the passage quoted on p. 40, Paul was reacting to *some* sense of delay. The very fact that some Christians had died and the end had not yet come required explanation. This is perhaps the first example of Christian theological adaptation.

Others reacted rather differently. They stressed still further the great benefits which they had already received through Christ. They already had the new life, the kingdom was among them, the Spirit filled them. What did it matter if the Lord did not physically return? Already he dwelt in them and they in him. Paul had, as we have seen, already taught along these lines. The writer of the Gospel of John was to make it the focus to which his belief constantly returned.

In his work, the future hardly features. Jesus himself had brought the great transition from the old world to the new, and in him judgement and resurrection had come upon the human scene. 'This is the judgement, that the light *has come* into the world, and men loved darkness rather than light' (3:19). 'He who hears my word and believes him who sent me . . . *has passed* from death to life' (5:24).

The writer of the Pastoral Epistles (probably at about the same date) criticises those who take this line too far, 'by holding that the resurrection is past already' (2 Tim. 2:18). For himself, he prefers a more balanced view. 'The appearing of our Lord Jesus Christ...will be made manifest at the proper time by the blessed and only Sovereign, the King of kings and Lord of lords' (1 Tim. 6:14 – 15). Meanwhile, the stress is on Christ as exalted to heaven and reigning there.

Whatever the method, clearly the early followers of Jesus did not lose their faith because the future programme was not fulfilled as their writings show they had first expected. That must mean that its details and even its whole shape were not quite as fundamental for them as they look. There was an element in that language of theirs which we should call poetic or figurative rather than literal (though whether they would have appreciated such a distinction is quite another matter). Their conviction was in the reality and power of God, to love and to save, made known through Jesus. That conviction remained stable (though it received new forms of expression), even when the earliest ways of putting some aspects of it were not matched by events. Christians continued to hope for future perfection, whether in life after death or in a return of Christ on some more distant, unknown day. The story of human life, including Christian human life, always needs an ending.

8
What did they believe about the church?

Many people are more familiar with the church than with Christianity. After all, it is the Christian society, with its officers, the clergy, and its buildings, which most obviously presents itself to our view. What is more, it is more noticeable in the country than in the cities, with its places of worship often dominating the landscape and reminding us of a long and rich history.

The picture was different in the early years. It is true that in the very first days in Palestine some Christians may well have been wandering country preachers, on the model of Jesus. But soon the church was virtually confined to towns. By the end of the first century it was to be found in most of the major cities of the eastern Mediterranean, particularly in Greece, Turkey (then Asia Minor), and Syria, besides some places in Egypt and Italy, including Rome, the capital of the Empire. But if you visited one of these towns and asked for 'the church', you would certainly not have been directed to any building. At this time, the Christians met in one another's houses, probably in the largest house available in the city. In Colossians 4:15, Paul sends his 'greetings to the brethren at Laodicea, and to Nympha and the church in her house.'

Did this community have leaders, anybody corresponding to the modern clergy? Certainly it did, though their titles and functions varied from place to place. From early days, it seems that they were even paid or maintained by the other Christians. In 1 Corinthians 9:15, Paul boasts that he has not made use of his right to payment, and sees his behaviour as exceptional. And in the later 1 Timothy (5:17), we read that good elders should be entitled to a double stipend.

This reference is to the leaders of a local congregation. In 1 Timothy 3, we read something of the characteristics required of these men. Already we find a quite elaborate set of regulations. Later in the same writing (ch. 5), we have rules for the older women of the congregation. Clearly organisation was in the air.

But in the first years, the leaders had a wider and more general role. They were called 'apostles', a word meaning 'someone sent out', that is 'emissary' or 'missionary'. Some were men who had been Jesus' companions from the first, like Peter and John, and Jesus' brother James (Gal. 2:9). But the most effective of them was Paul, who became a Christian a few years after Jesus' death, having been a vigorous opponent of the church. It was largely because of him that the church spread so quickly, not only into non-Jewish lands but among non-Jewish people. He saw from the start that what God had done and taught through Jesus applied to everybody, not just to Jews among whom he had lived and worked. It was God's word for the human race.

Paul the Jew saw this in two ways. First, he saw in Jesus a kind of fresh start for human life in relation to God. Jesus was a new Adam (see p. 32). This meant that in the church, people of all kinds could be accepted equally, for Adam was the father not just of Jews but of all mankind. Paul wrote, 'There is neither Jew nor Greek, there is neither slave nor free, there is neither male nor female; for you are all one in Christ Jesus' (Gal. 3:28). It is hard to overestimate the power of those words. Whatever inequalities existed in people's ordinary lives in society, this doctrine meant that in the setting of the church, which for the converts became the main focus of their lives, it was quite different.

This setting up of a two-tier style of life (being both in the church and in society) was not without its problems, and we can see Paul arriving at diplomatic compromises and smoothing over awkward situations. For example, though Paul can say that in Christ 'there is neither male nor female', he was not happy that the women in the congregation at Corinth should interrupt the preacher with questions. 'Let them ask their husbands at home' (1 Cor. 14:35). And though he says that in Christ 'there is neither slave nor free', he does not go so far as to condemn the system of slavery outright, but urges slaves to obey their masters, and indeed urges masters to treat their slaves justly, 'knowing that you also have a Master in heaven' (Col. 3:22 – 4:1). (It has to be realised that slavery at that time was a much more diverse and generally less offensive institution than it has often been in more recent times. It has fewer of the overtones of cruelty, powerlessness and poverty.)

Second, Paul still set great store by the church's Jewish roots. New it might be from many points of view, but it was still related to God's people, Israel, from which it had sprung.

It was not simply that some of its ways of organising itself were similar to those of Judaism (so that a stranger in Corinth or Ephesus who perhaps directed you to the synagogue when you asked for the church made an understandable mistake). Nor was it simply that there was a factual, historical link. It was also that the church felt itself to be in some sense the heir or fulfilment of Judaism, the true Israel.

Christians differed on how exactly to express the relationship. Some saw the church as enjoying the fulfilment of God's promises of old to his people, but believed that the Jews, most of whom were so far unwilling to acknowledge this fact, would soon rally to the Christian flag, realising their God-given destiny Paul saw the future in these terms, 'I want you to understand this mystery, brethren: a hardening has come upon part of Israel, until the full number of the Gentiles come in, and so all Israel will be saved' (Rom. 11:25).

Others regarded the Jews as now abandoned by God. They had rejected and crucified Jesus their Messiah and the church had wholly succeeded to their inheritance. In Mark 12:1 – 12 we read a parable which expresses such a view. And in Matthew 23 we can see something of the bitterness with which some Christians regarded the leaders of Jewish opinion, with whom they were in intense conflict.

Others again took a gentler view. The stories of Jesus' birth in Luke 1 – 2 show him coming into a warm, welcoming Jewish setting. Notice the portraits of Zechariah and Elizabeth, Mary and Joseph, Simeon and Anna. The whole of Luke's Gospel and Acts, two parts of a single work, portrays a Jewish background to Jesus and the church which was not wholly hostile and which provided a necessary foundation upon which the church was built.

But as Christians thought about the society which had come from Jesus and which was rapidly growing and spreading and so finding its own identity, they did not consider only their relation to Israel. Chiefly, they thought of themselves in relation to Jesus himself. How did this relationship strike them?

Most obviously, he was their founder. But to leave it at that would be to fail utterly to describe their belief about themselves as a community deriving from him. Some of them (again Paul is the most striking and influential) saw the church as having no life independent of him. It lived on his resources, was attached to him, was part of him, was 'in' him. Paul used striking images to convey this belief. The church was Christ's body, or his bride. 'Just as the body is one and has many members...so it is with Christ' (1 Cor. 12:12).

Paul was not unique. Other writers followed suit. In John 15 we read, 'I am the vine, you are the branches' (v.5). This image had been used in the Old Testament (see especially Isaiah 5) for Israel, tended and cared for by God. So it combined neatly the two main aspects of early Christian belief about the church: it had inherited the mantle of Israel, and it depended wholly on Christ. Also, he was the link between the two, for he was God's agent sent to his people to fulfil his purposes.

9
What did they do about worship?

Reading this book so far, and especially its title and chapter headings, you might think that being an early Christian was chiefly a matter of believing certain things, or believing in God in a certain way. That is, you might suppose they were a rather intellectual collection of people, like a network of discussion groups or political cells.

That impression is misleading. Christian life centred on the practical service of God, in both worship and moral living. To make the point, we have put the word 'do' instead of 'believe' in the title of this chapter.

How did the first Christians worship God? The evidence, such as it is (it is not a subject they wrote much about), points to their having continued in the ways of the synagogue. They read the Old Testament scriptures, prayed and preached. But, as in all other respects, the picture had been transformed as a result of Jesus. This happened in a number of ways.

In the first place, they looked at the old scriptures in the light of Jesus, that is, they read them as prophecy fulfilled. Some passages lent themselves to this interpretation more than others. It is likely that in discussion and in controversy with Jews, and probably in their own worship, they gave special attention to these passages. Some of them were so illuminating that they even coloured the way in which they told the story of Jesus' life on earth. You have only to read Psalm 22 alongside the story of Jesus' trial and death as told in Mark 14 – 15 to see the point. Here is one example,

And they crucified him, and divided his garments among them, casting lots for them, to decide what each should take (Mark 15:24).

They divide my garments among them, and for my raiment they cast lots (Ps. 22:18).

In the second place, they prayed to Jesus, as well as to God himself. The oldest Christian prayer known to us, *maranatha* (1 Cor. 16:22), is Aramaic (the common native language of Palestine in the time of Jesus) for 'Our Lord, come'. It shows us not only that they felt free to address Jesus, now exalted to heaven, but also how prominent was that hope for his return which we described in chapter 7.

Their prayer was corporate. It was a matter for the community, as the opening of the model prayer, '*Our* Father' (Matt. 6:9) shows. It may seem strange not to call this the oldest prayer known to us, for surely it was given by Jesus himself. Strictly speaking, however, it comes to us in two slightly different forms, in the Gospels of Matthew (6:9 – 13) and Luke (11:2 – 4), and it is uncertain which of these two forms, if indeed either of them precisely, goes back to Jesus.

The teaching on prayer given in Matthew 6, which deals with personal devotions and seems to imply that private prayer is to be preferred to public, is probably not about that issue at all. Rather, like the teaching in the second half of the previous chapter, it is concerned chiefly to urge single-mindedness and integrity of inner motive. You must not pray with an eye on impressing other people with your piety. Jewish teaching on prayer was similar.

But it was not simply the content and object of prayer which took on a fresh appearance. Two religious rites became characteristic of the Christians, probably from earliest days: baptism and communion. Both have their ancestry in Jewish custom, both acquired a wholly new meaning, and both have remained at the centre of Christian practice from that day to this.

Because of social exclusiveness on the part of the better off members of the congregation at Corinth in the early fifties, Paul writes to recall them to the basis of their gatherings and of their solemn meal together.

> For I received from the Lord what I also delivered to you, that the Lord Jesus on the night when he was betrayed took bread, and when he had given thanks, he broke it, and said, 'This is my body which is for you. Do this in remembrance of me.' In the same way also the cup, after supper, saying 'This cup is the new covenant in my blood. Do this, as often as you drink it, in remembrance of me' (1 Cor. 11:23 – 25).

This meal, reminding them directly of Jesus' sacrificial death, was the sign and expression of their fellowship, centred on Jesus. 'The bread which we break, is it not a sharing in the body of Christ?' (1 Cor. 10:16). The Gospels of Mark, Matthew and Luke, written a few years later, also recall that meal as part of the story of Jesus' last day with his followers, no doubt because it played such an important part in the background to the regular practice of the church.

But it was not simply a recalling of the sad events of that day. It also expressed their awareness of his living presence with them and of their hope for the future. 'For as often as you eat this bread and drink this cup, you proclaim the Lord's death until he comes,' Paul continues after describing the supper. The moving story of the walk to Emmaus on the first day of the week, finishing with Jesus making himself known to the two disciples 'in the breaking of the bread' (Luke 24:13 – 35), was surely told with regular, continuing practice of the communion meal or the eucharist in mind. (The rite was soon called 'eucharist' because its central act is the *giving of thanks* (Greek *eucharistia* means 'thanksgiving') over the bread and wine.) We know that, from as early as Paul's time, Christians were meeting on the first day of the week, associated with Jesus' resurrection.

Then there was baptism. How were new converts to be incorporated into the church? Judaism already had the rite of plunging people into water as a sign of transition to a new state of life, whether they were Gentiles wishing to become linked to Judaism, or monks at Qumran wishing to keep themselves prepared for God's coming great day, or hearers of John the Baptist similarly wanting to repent and be ready. The practice lay to hand, and it was not surprising that the church adopted it as the usual means of introducing new believers. But for Christians, its significance centred wholly on Christ. It was not so much the way of joining the church, as it has often come to be regarded, as of entering into Christ's very experience of death and resurrection. We have already seen how Paul regarded it in those terms (p. 29). This view of it was prompted probably by the very nature of the act (going down into water and emerging), and it was nourished by the memory of the miraculous crossing of the Red Sea by the people of Israel under Moses, to which Jews looked back as their great national moment of redemption.

The death of Jesus had taken place at the time of Passover, the Jewish festival which commemorated that great episode in Jewish history. It is probable that the last supper, on which the church's eucharist was modelled, was in fact the meal of the Passover taken together by Jewish households. So once more in these two rites of baptism and eucharist, Jewish past and Christian present fuse together in the life of the first Christians.

Our evidence of what early Christian worship was like is sparse, and the closest glimpse of it may not be typical. It comes in 1 Corinthians 14, where, as in the case of the meal, it is the problem of disorder which leads to the record being available for us. If all had been well, Paul would have had no reason to refer to the matter. We are given a picture of a high degree of religious emotion, with preaching and praying both in ordinary speech and in ecstatic, unintelligible utterance. The atmosphere is what we should call charismatic. It reads as if there was ample scope for private initiative. Paul was attempting to bring greater order and discipline.

Apart from that precious glimpse, perhaps our most immediate contact with early Christian worship is in certain hymns and other forms which happen to have been incorporated into longer writings. For example, the suggestion has been made that Philippians 2:6 – 11 is in fact a hymn about Christ which Paul included in his letter to support his encouragement of the virtue of humility. It makes clear how strongly the prayer of those Christians centred on the figure of Jesus himself, 'to the glory of God the Father'.

10
What did they believe about right and wrong?

Where do we get our beliefs about right and wrong? Not usually from a single, clearly defined authority, but from a wide variety of sources. Some we pick up without ever thinking them out, as if from the air around us. They are part of the culture we inherit from our parents and others close to us. That is how we come to think it good to show gratitude, tell the truth, and refrain from injuring people. Others come to us from the character of someone we admire, whether we know them from life or from books. Others again from the law of the land. We discover it is wrong to drive at high speeds on motorways or to bring a stray dog back with us from the continent. Finally, we come to feel some kinds of behaviour are wrong because they fly in the face of some deep principle which we have come to hold. We feel it is simply intolerable to torture people for their political opinions and to be other than considerate to the sick or the aged.

The first Christians derived their morality, their beliefs about right and wrong, from sources of all these kinds. They took over lists of vices which would have been condemned by most thinking people in the world of the time (most of them, though not all, by people at almost any time). The end of the first chapter of Paul's letter to the Romans is an example. In the same way, they shared with those around them a sense of the rightness of obligations between members of households, husbands and wives, parents and children, masters and slaves. Lists of such duties appear in a number of New Testament writings, for example in Colossians 3:18 – 4:1.

From their Jewish background they inherited a full-scale body of laws, regulating every aspect of life. It was available for them, ready-made. Some of them were happy to take it over in full as the basis for their own system of morality. The Gospel of Matthew portrays Jesus teaching precisely this,

> For truly I say to you, till heaven and earth pass away, not an iota, not a dot, will pass from the law until all is accomplished. Whoever then relaxes one of the least of these commandments and teaches men so, shall be called least in the kingdom of heaven (Matt. 5:18 – 19).

Others, however, and notably Paul, were not happy with this. He saw Jesus' coming as bringing to an end the whole regime of the Jewish law. Much of that law was concerned, not with social and personal morals, but with the regulation of worship and with keeping strict boundaries between Jews and non-Jews. Paul believed this distinction to be at an end. God had now established in Jesus a new basis for man's relationship with him. So it could not be that the law should be taken over lock, stock and barrel. Paul abandoned its ritual provision and its boundary-making rules, while continuing to commend its fundamental moral aspects. Thus, he quotes the latter part of the Ten Commandments, derived from Exodus 20, in Romans 13:9.

Whatever their approach to the Law, early Christians seem to have agreed on one ethical matter which was a new departure. They gave priority to the command to love. This became the overriding principle, affecting the way all other rules and regulations were applied.

But whom was one to love? That question receives a number of different answers. Paul is content to quote Leviticus 19:18, in the Jewish law, and he puts it forward as summing up the whole of morality. 'Love is the fulfilling of the law' (Rom. 13:10). In its original context, this command applies to one's fellow-Israelites. Paul omits to say who he takes the neighbour to be and we cannot be sure what he had in mind.

In the Gospel of Mark, Jesus gives the same command, but he puts it alongside a first command, taken from Deuteronomy (6:5), 'You shall love the Lord your God' (Mark 12:30). Then he says, 'There is no other commandment greater than these.' This two-fold duty of love is to be the key to all behaviour; but again the extent of love for the neighbour is not specified.

But in the Gospels of Matthew and Luke that omission is repaired. 'I say to you love your enemies' (Matt. 5:44). Here is a new, revolutionary standard, which Jesus then goes on to spell out in detail.

Similarly, in Luke 10, when the scribe asks, 'Who is my neighbour?' he is given the story of the Good Samaritan. To understand its power, we need to know that in acting generously to the abandoned traveller, presumably a Jew, the Samaritan, a member of the schismatic, outcast group in Israel, goes right beyond what could be expected of him. He even risks ritual contamination from touching what might turn out to be a corpse, a risk avoided by the priest and levite, who thus at a certain level do their duty.

Love, then, extends to any one in need, even to your enemy. The quality of love is thus being defined anew, to include the kind of care and generosity which situations such as that described in the parable can evoke.

One Christian group looked at the matter in another way. In the Gospel of John, the command to love one's neighbour does not appear. Instead, we read, 'A new commandment I give to you, that you love one another' (13:34). Here, love is seen as the bond of the Christian community itself. What is more, this command, repeated a number of times, is the only piece of teaching on right and wrong to be found in this Gospel. It gives us no help at all with moral problems (such as divorce and the rightness of possessing property) which we know from elsewhere preoccupied many early Christians. Instead, we have simply, 'Love one another'.

11
What does it matter
what they believed?

A reader brought up in the cultural tradition of the countries
in which the Christian faith has been dominant over the
centuries would almost certainly find himself on reasonably
familiar territory in reading about the early Christians'
beliefs. He might not accept the truth of any of the beliefs
described. He might find some of them attractive, others
outlandish. But, unless he were wholly unaware of many
aspects of the culture within which he lived, he would feel the
pattern as a whole to be part of his heritage. From the point
of view of the cultural tradition of the western world, there is
no doubt about the deep formative role of these beliefs.

On the other hand, even if he were involved in the
Christian church of our day, our reader might well have
received a jolt at certain points in the account given in this
book. This is because even patterns of belief firmly held by an
orgainised body develop over the years and adjust themselves
to changed conditions. Strangeness and familiarity, change
from the past and continuity over the years—some observers
will be inclined to emphasise the one, some the other. Neither
can reasonably be forgotten.

The reader who is a Christian believer will be most likely to
feel the force of the belief of the first Christians. He will have
least difficulty in identifying with them. He shares with them
common allegiance to God, made known through Jesus, and
to Jesus himself as the one who brought the new relationship
with God and all that it entailed. Like them, he knows the
rewards and responsibilities of membership of the church.

Like them, he worships God through Bible and eucharist, and he sets about applying the morality of love in his daily life. Even if some of the New Testament language sounds strange to him, he will be able to identify the experience it reflects and share its insight into such problems as he has in common with the earliest Christians. His continuity with them yields all that undoubted fruit.

Where the believer may find difficulty is in underestimating the differences between his position and that of the first Christians, the developments which have occurred, and the continuing need for adaptation and re-expression if the faith is to retain its power to convince.

It is possible, and it has been attempted in this book, to face the distinctiveness of the past, looking at it, as far as possible, in its own right. If we see it in this way, we may be freed from the instinct to shape it according to our preferences, and then it will be able to stimulate our own imagination in such a way as to make us look afresh at the task of believing now.

After all, the dynamic faith of the first Christians gives us our clue. They believed in the sovereign rule of God and the power of his Spirit among them. Sharing that belief, which Jesus had planted in them and which he continued to nourish, means seeking continually the best ways of accepting that rule and responding to that ever-present inspiration.

But may the beliefs of the first Christians matter in any deeper way? What the first Christians believed matters, at the deepest level, only if what they stood for, and the life and faith which come from them, strike us as truth. It matters if we see their beliefs as opening a door, which leads us to understand God's ways and our own life with new clarity. Then believing comes alive for us, and we stretch hands out to those who first believed and who helped us on the way.